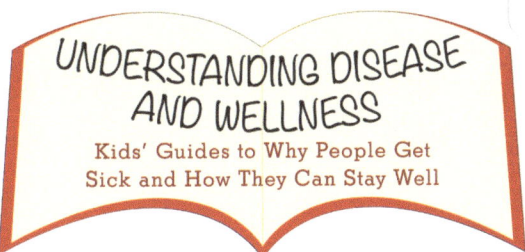

UNDERSTANDING DISEASE AND WELLNESS
Kids' Guides to Why People Get Sick and How They Can Stay Well

A KID'S GUIDE TO DIABETES

Series List

A Kid's Guide to a Healthier You
A Kid's Guide to AIDS and HIV
A Kid's Guide to Allergies
A Kid's Guide to Asthma
A Kid's Guide to Bugs and How They Can Make You Sick
A Kid's Guide to Cancer
A Kid's Guide to Diabetes
A Kid's Guide to Drugs and Alcohol
A Kid's Guide to Immunizations
A Kid's Guide to Malnutrition
A Kid's Guide to Obesity
A Kid's Guide to Pollution and How It Can Make You Sick
A Kid's Guide to Viruses and Bacteria

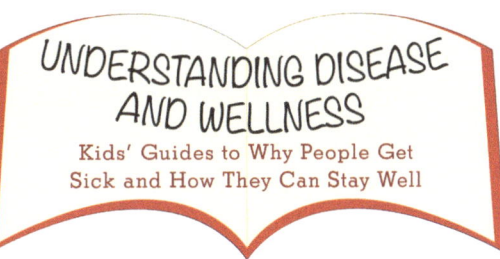

A KID'S GUIDE TO DIABETES

Rae Simons

Understanding Disease and Wellness:
Kids' Guides to Why People Get Sick and How They Can Stay Well
A KID'S GUIDE TO DIABETES

Copyright © 2016 by Village Earth Press, a division of Harding House Publishing. All rights reserved. No part of this publication may be reproduced or transmitted in any form or by any means, electronic or mechanical, including photocopying, recording, taping, or any information storage and retrieval system, without permission from the publisher.

Village Earth Press
Vestal, New York 13850
www.villageearthpress.com

First Printing
9 8 7 6 5 4 3 2 1

Series ISBN (paperback): 978-1-62524-445-1
ISBN (paperback): 978-1-62524-415-4
ebook ISBN: 978-1-62524-050-7
Library of Congress Control Number: 2013911243

Author: Simons, Rae

Note: This book is a revised and updated edition of *Kids & Diabetes* (ISBN: 978-1-934970-17-1), published in 2009 by Alpha House Publishing.

Introduction

According to a recent study reported in the Virginia Henderson International Nursing Library, kids worry about getting sick. They worry about AIDS and cancer, about allergies and the "super-germs" that resist medication. They know about these ills—but they don't always understand what causes them or how they can be prevented.

Unfortunately, most 9- to 11-year-olds, the study found, get their information about diseases like AIDS from friends and television; only 20 percent of the children interviewed based their understanding of illness on facts they had learned at school. Too often, kids believe urban legends, schoolyard folktales, and exaggerated movie plots. Oftentimes, misinformation like this only makes their worries worse. The January 2008 *Child Health News* reported that 55 percent of all children between 9 and 13 "worry almost all the time" about illness.

This series, **Understanding Disease and Wellness**, offers readers clear information on various illnesses and conditions, as well as the immunizations that can prevent many diseases. The books dispel the myths with clearly presented facts and colorful, accurate illustrations. Better yet, these books will help kids understand not only illness—but also what they can do to stay as healthy as possible.

—*Dr. Elise Berlan*

Just the Facts

- Your body needs insulin to make sugars into energy. When you have diabetes, you don't have enough insulin, and sugars build up in your body.

- Type 1 diabetes appears in children or teenagers, while type 2 diabetes appears later in life.

- Symptoms of diabetes include extreme thirst, extreme hunger, weight loss, fatigue, blurred vision, and slow-healing sores or infections.

- People with diabetes can live normal lives, but need to monitor their blood-sugar levels; people with type 1 diabetes and some people with type 2 diabetes use insulin shots or patches to keep their blood-sugar levels normal.

- By exercising and eating a variety of fruits and vegetables you can help prevent diabetes.

- Both type 1 and type 2 diabetes can run in families, but eating foods with a lot of sugar or foods that are high in fat puts you at risk for diabetes too.

- Obesity has been linked to diabetes. Losing weight lowers blood-sugar levels and makes people less likely to get diabetes.

- Diabetes is a problem around the world. Many people in poorer countries don't know they have diabetes or have fewer treatment options.

- By exercising and eating a variety of fruits and vegetables you can help prevent diabetes.

What Is Diabetes?

You've probably heard about people with diabetes. You may know somone who has this disease—or you may have this disease yourself. You probably know that many people with diabetes have to give themselves shots. But you may not understand what diabetes is.

Diabetes isn't an illness like the flu or a cold, where a virus or another germ has invaded your body. Instead, it's a condition caused by a part of your body not working properly.

Did You Know?

As many as 7 percent of the world's people have diabetes. That means if you were to have a hundred people in a room, the odds are that seven of them would have diabetes. According to the World Health Organization, in 2012, there were 347 million people in the world with this disease, and that number is still climbing.

Normally, your body changes most of the food you eat into glucose (a form of sugar), so that you can use it for the energy you need to live and move. Insulin is a *hormone* produced by an *organ* in your body called the pancreas that allows glucose to enter all the cells of your body and be used as energy. When you have diabetes, however, your body doesn't make enough insulin or can't use insulin properly. This allows sugar to build up in your blood instead of moving into the cells. Some, but not all, of the extra sugar is carried out of your body (through your urine when you go to the bathroom), and the energy is wasted.

Words to Know

Hormone: a chemical substance produced in the body that controls and regulates certain body activities.

Organ: a part of the body that carries out a particular job or function (such as your lungs or heart).

What Is Sugar?

We all know that sugar is that white, sweet stuff. It's also a chemical made from oxygen, carbon, and hydrogen *molecules* combined in a certain way. A special kind of sugar—glucose—is very important to our bodies. Glucose gives our bodies energy.

This type of sugar comes from breaking down carbohydrates into a chemical our bodies can easily change into energy. This happens when the bonds that otherwise hold the molecules together are broken inside these chemicals.

Words to Know

Molecules: the smallest particles of a substance that have all the chemical and physical properties of that substance. Molecules are made up of two or more atoms.

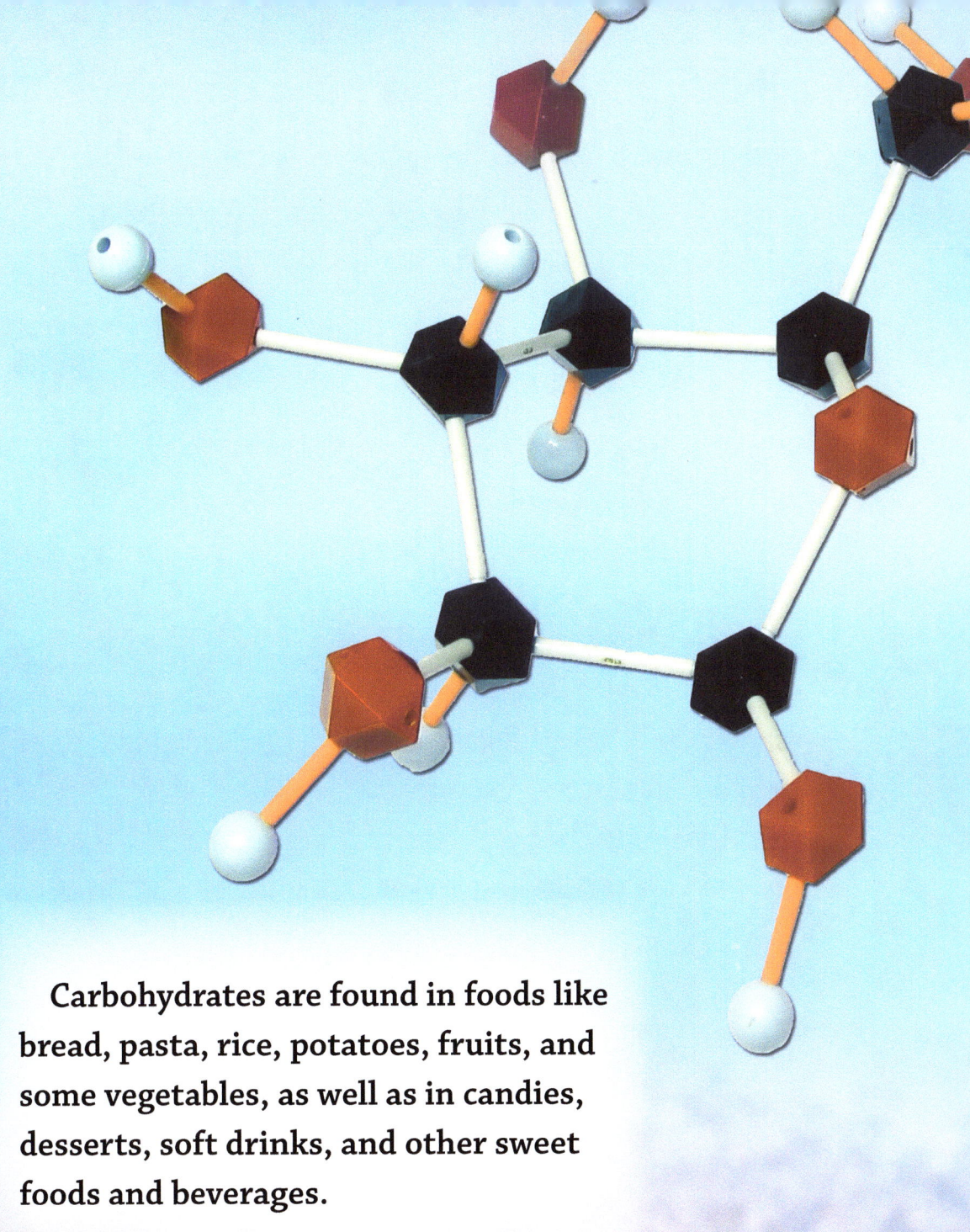

Carbohydrates are found in foods like bread, pasta, rice, potatoes, fruits, and some vegetables, as well as in candies, desserts, soft drinks, and other sweet foods and beverages.

How Does Your Body Break Down Sugar?

Sugar is broken down inside your body in two main places: your muscles and your liver.

In your liver, a hormone called glucagon is what makes this chemical reaction happen. The level of sugar in your blood is what tells your liver to release this hormone.

Did You Know?

Glucose, the kind of sugar your body uses, occurs naturally in the sap of most plants and in the juice from fruit. Glucose is a normal part of animal blood, which is why it doesn't need to be digested any more before being absorbed into the bloodstream.

When your blood sugar level is low, the hormone is *secreted* and breaks down the sugar into simpler chemicals. Now it can enter the blood and get sugar levels back to normal. Meanwhile, as your muscles contract and move, they stimulate sugar breakdown. This gives your muscles the energy they need. Since your muscles don't have an endless supply of stored sugar, you eventually run out of "fuel." After exercising, your body needs to rebuild its supply, so it uses the sugar in your bloodstream. Once this sugar is lowered, it once again triggers your liver to do its job.

Words to Know

Liver: an organ in the upper part of your belly that breaks down sugar and removes waste products and worn-out cells from the blood. The liver is the largest solid organ in the body, weighing in at about three and a half pounds.

Secreted: produced and released a substance.

Pancreas

Your pancreas is another organ that's very important in the way your body uses sugar.

The pancreas is about 6 inches (15 cm) long, and it's shaped a little like a fish. It stretches across the back of your *abdomen,* behind your stomach. The head of the pancreas is on the right side of the abdomen and is connected to the duodenum (the first section of the small intestine). The narrow end of the pancreas, called the tail, extends to the left side of your body.

The pancreas makes pancreatic juices and hormones, including insulin. The pancreatic juices contain chemicals that help digest food in the small intestine. Insulin controls the amount of sugar in the blood, which is very important to how your body uses sugar.

ASK THE DOCTOR

My grandfather had a tumor on his pancreas and had to have part of his pancreas removed. Will he be able to live without it?

A: Yes, people can live without part of their pancreas. However, your grandfather will probably need to take insulin now, as the part of his pancreas that is left will not be able to make all that he needs.

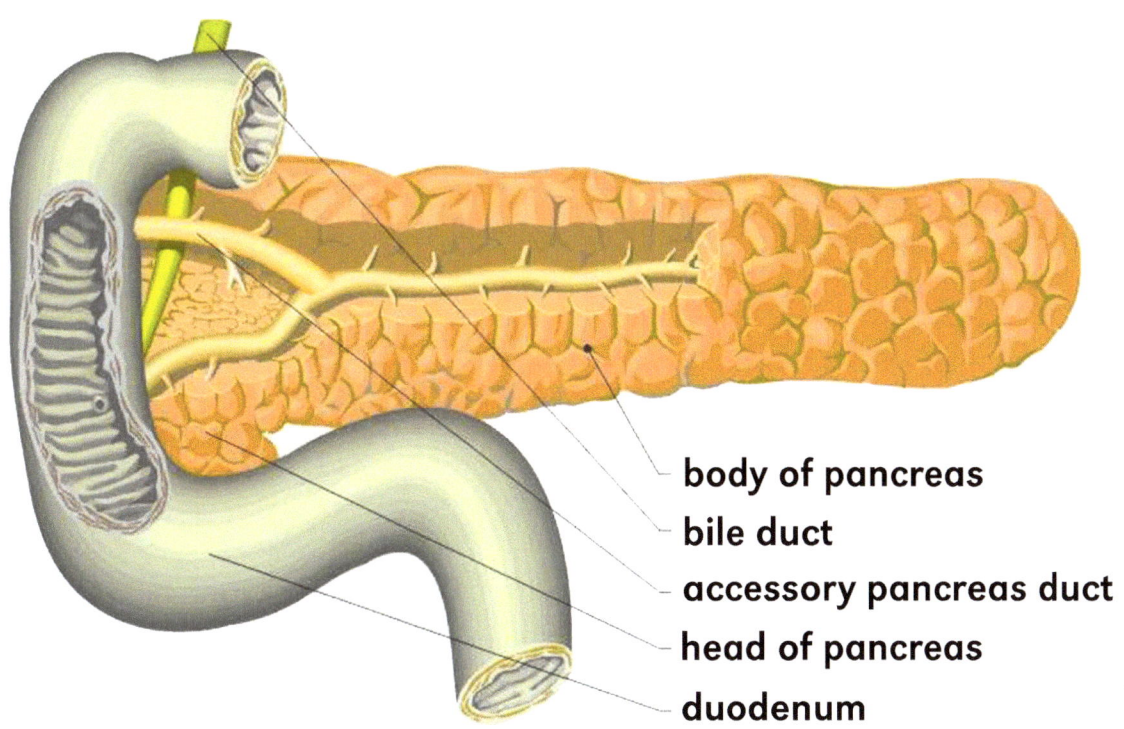

- body of pancreas
- bile duct
- accessory pancreas duct
- head of pancreas
- duodenum

Words to Know

Abdomen: the belly, the part of the body between the chest and the hips, which contains many important body organs.

Ducts: passageways for carrying a fluid or substance from one site to another.

The pancreas's *ducts* connect it to both the liver and the small intestine. If any part of the pancreas isn't doing its job, digestion and insulin production will not take place normally.

Islets of Langerhans

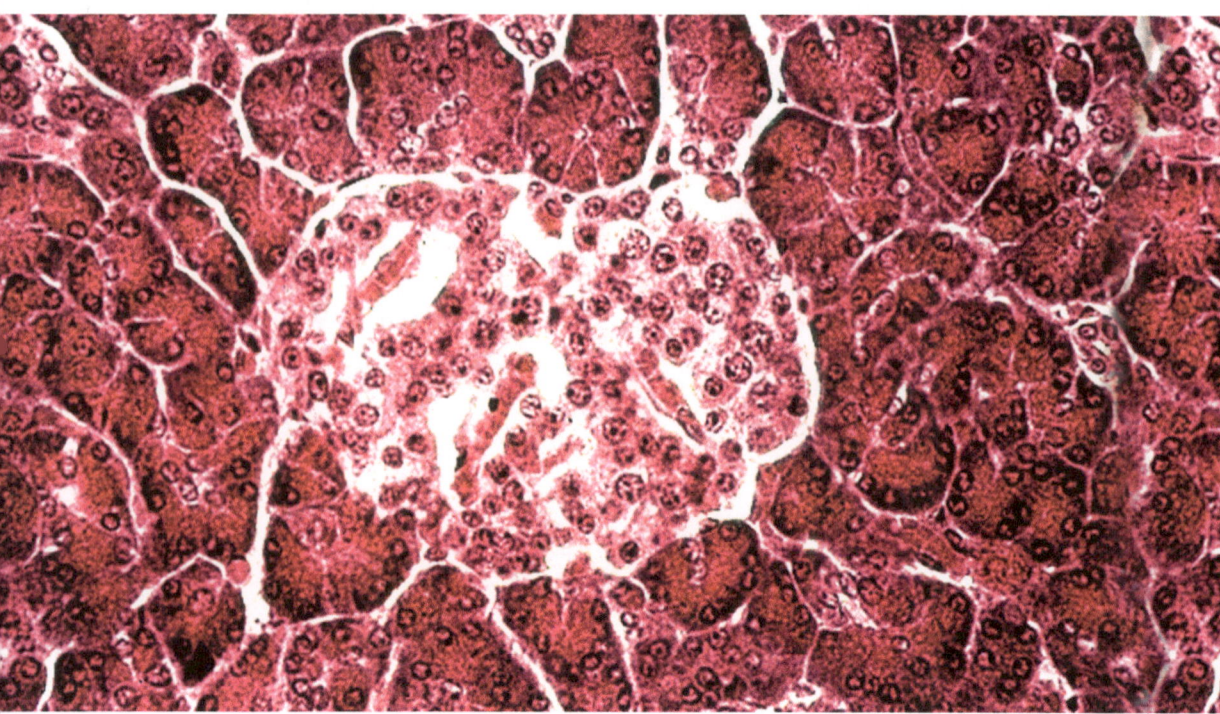

The islets of Langerhans (shown through a microscope above) are special groups of *beta cells* in the pancreas. These are the cells that make and secrete insulin to break down blood sugar. (They were named after Paul Langerhans, the German scientist who discovered them in 1869.) The picture to the right shows the connection between the pancreas, insulin production, and the glucose available to muscles for energy.

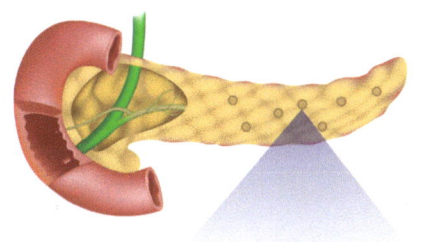

Pancreas

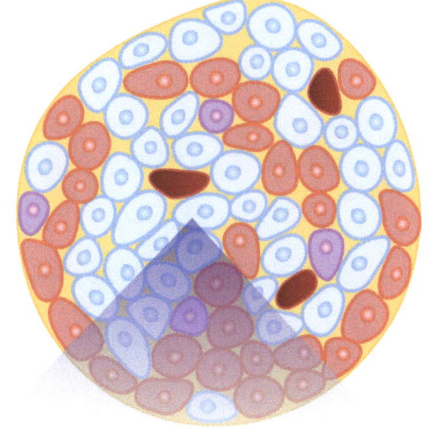

Pancreatic islet

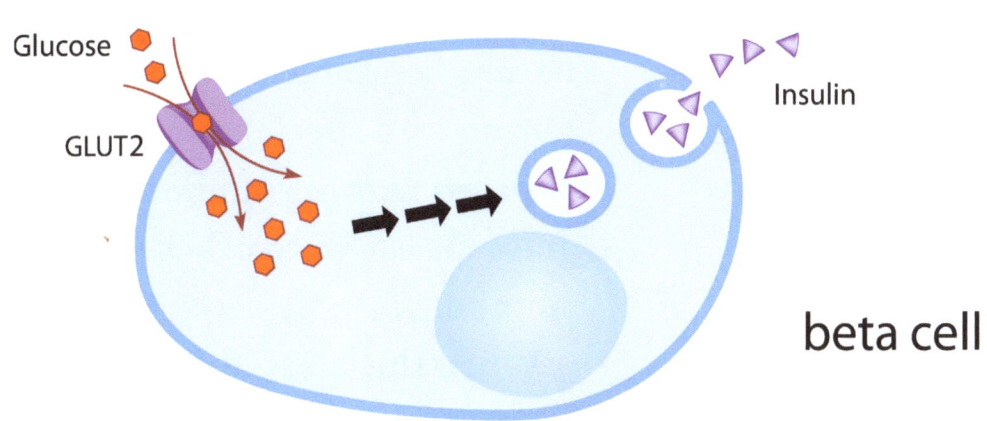

beta cell

Words to Know

Beta Cell: beta cells make and release insulin.

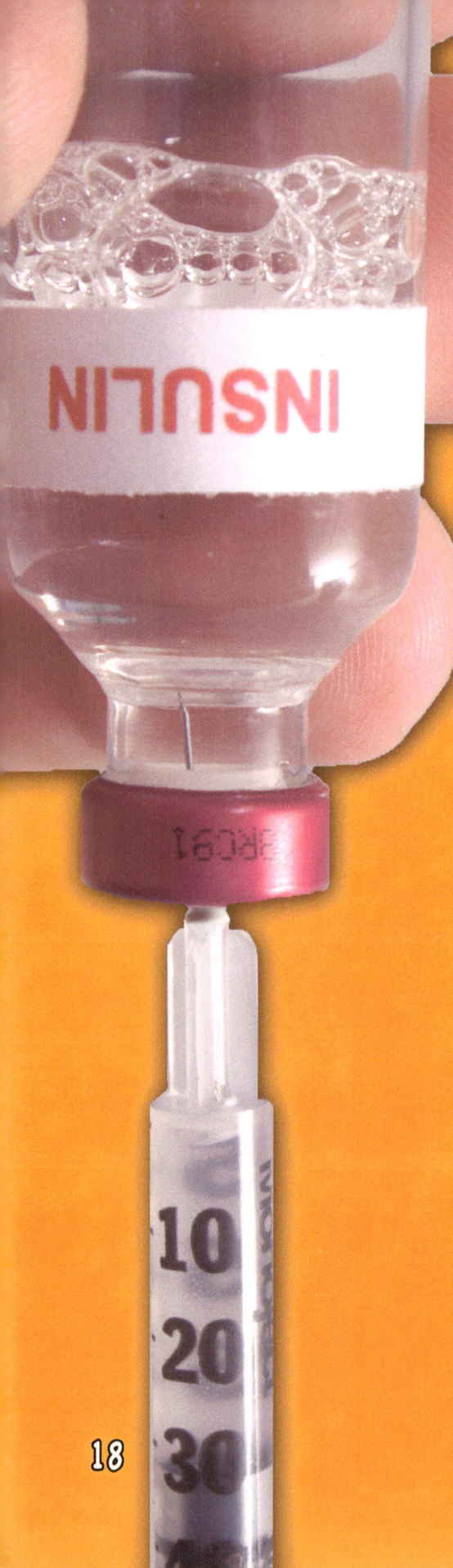

Insulin

If you know someone who is a diabetic, you may have seen insulin in little bottles that is drawn out by hypodermic needles, as shown to the left. However, insulin is also a chemical that your body naturally produces. It's a hormone, a special chemical released within your body that gives messages to other parts of your body.

When the islets of Langerhans get the message that sugar levels in the blood are high, they release insulin. Most cells in your body have insulin receptors, special chemical hook-up sites that can fasten on to the insulin that's now circulating through your blood. When a cell has insulin attached to its surface, the cell signals other receptors, which then absorb sugar from the blood-stream into the inside of the cell. Now the cell can use the sugar for the energy it needs to carry out all the processes that give you life.

People who don't naturally have enough insulin in their bodies have diabetes. They usually need to take insulin, often in the form of shots. This insulin used to come from cows and pigs. It worked just fine for most people who needed insulin, but a few people were allergic to it. Today, scientists have found a way to create human insulin artificially, using bacteria and cloning techniques. Big vats of bacteria now make all the human insulin needed.

Words to Know

Bacteria: tiny, one-celled creatures. Some are harmful and cause disease, but many are helpful.

Cloning: making multiple, identical copies of something using the cells' genetic material.

Did You Know?

Without insulin in your body, you could eat lots of food and still starve. Your body's cells cannot get to the energy contained in sugar without the help of insulin.

Type I Juvenile Diabetes

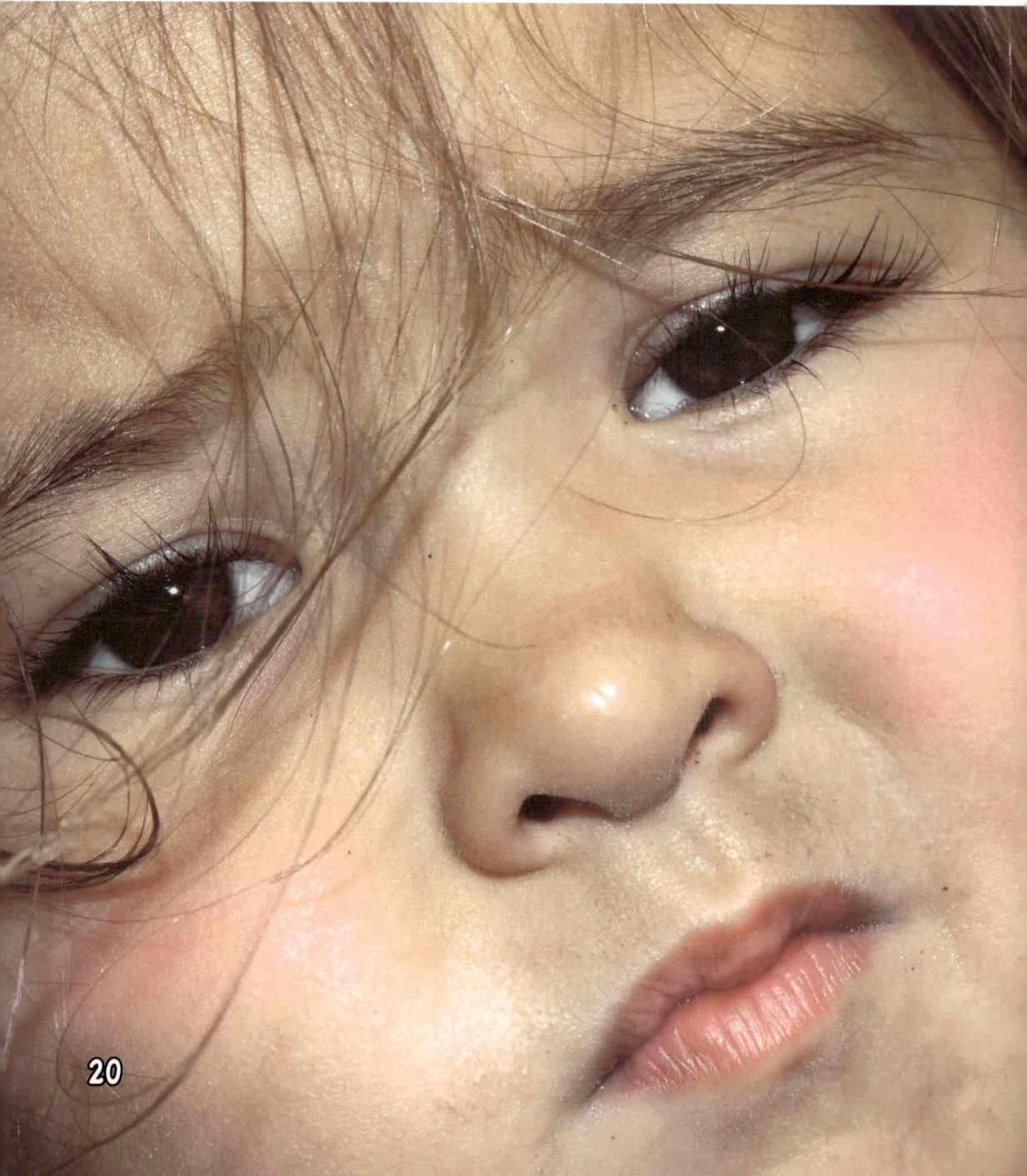

There are two forms of diabetes: type 1 (also often known as juvenile diabetes) and type 2.

Type 1 diabetes means the pancreas produces little or no insulin. Although type 1 diabetes can develop at any age, it typically appears during childhood or when a person is a teenager.

Various factors may contribute to type 1 diabetes, including a parent or grandparent who has this disease, or *exposure* to certain germs. There is no cure for type 1 diabetes. Once you have it, you will always have it, but with proper treatment, people who have type 1 diabetes can expect to live long, healthy lives.

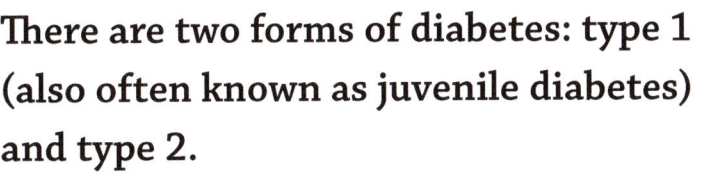

Words to Know

Exposure: in a state of being without protection.

Type 2 Diabetes

ASK THE DOCTOR

Why does being overweight and not exercising make you more apt to get type 2 diabetes? It doesn't make sense to me.

A: The more fatty tissue you have, the more resistant your cells become to insulin. Physical activity helps you control your weight and decreases fat, and it also uses up glucose as energy and makes your cells more sensitive to insulin.

If you have type 2 diabetes, either your body is resistant to the effects of insulin or your body doesn't produce enough insulin to keep your blood sugar levels where they need to be. Type 2 diabetes can often be prevented, but the condition is on the rise, mostly because there are so many more people who are *obese* than there once were.

Type 2 diabetes has no cure, but there's plenty people can do to both prevent and manage the condition. Eating healthy foods, exercising, and maintaining a healthy weight are all ways to keep from getting type 2 diabetes—and to control it if you have it. Sometimes, however, you may need insulin to manage your blood sugar.

Words to Know

Obese: having more body weight than is healthy.

Did You Know?

Doctors don't know why, but people of certain backgrounds—including Africans, Hispanics, North American Indians, and Asians—are more likely to develop type 2 diabetes.

Symptoms

Both type 1 and type 2 diabetes share the same symptoms:

Increased thirst and frequent urination. As sugar builds up in your bloodstream, fluid is pulled from your tissues. This leaves you thirsty, and you'll tend to drink and urinate more than usual.

Extreme hunger. Without enough insulin to move sugar into your cells, your muscles don't have enough energy. This makes you feel very hungry—and eating may not help.

Weight loss. Despite eating more than usual to *relieve* your constant hunger, you may lose weight. Without energy supplies, your fat and muscle tissues may shrink.

Fatigue. When your cells don't have enough sugar, you feel tired.

Blurred vision. If your blood sugar level is too high, fluid may be pulled from your tissues, including your eyes, which as a result, may not be able to focus.

Slow-healing sores or frequent infections. Diabetes affects your ability to heal and fight infections.

Words to Know

Relieve: to lessen, to free from pain.

Diagnosis

Blood tests are the first step your doctor will take if she thinks you might have diabetes. Usually, all she'll need to do is *prick* your finger.

These blood tests will tell your doctor what your blood sugar levels are, and this measures how well your body processes sugar. If the levels are too high, it indicates you have diabetes. Then your doctor will probably do more tests to figure out if you have type 1 or type 2 diabetes. The kind of treatment you will have depends on the type of diabetes you have.

Words to Know

Prick: a small, very quick piercing of the skin.

Living with Diabetes

When a person finds out he or she has diabetes, it's normal to feel sad, scared, and even angry. Diabetes is a serious disease, and it will mean that the person has to change the way he or she lives. There will be lots of new things to handle: new diet, new medicines, new devices, new habits. But people with diabetes can learn to cope with their disease and go on to live normal lives.

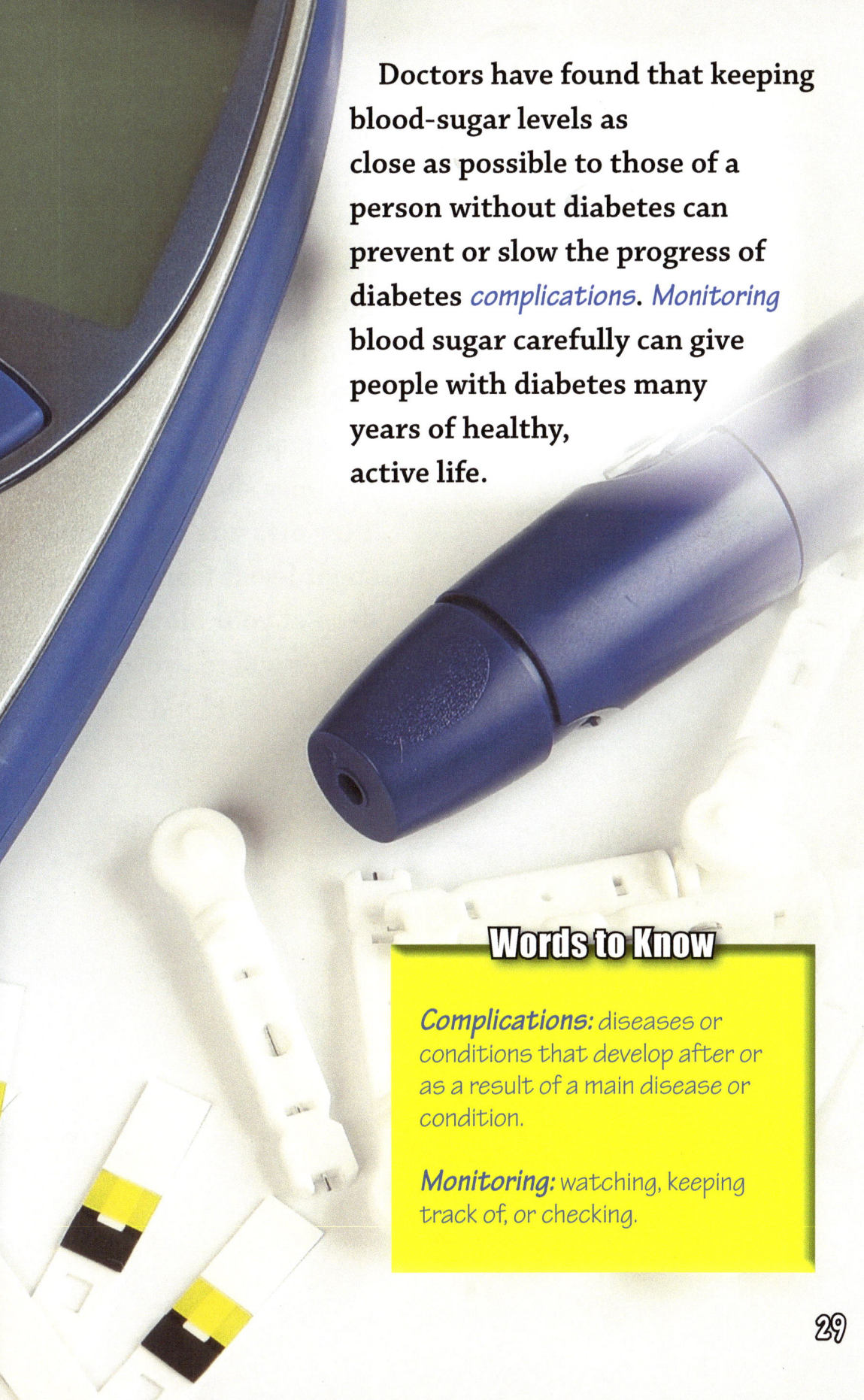

Doctors have found that keeping blood-sugar levels as close as possible to those of a person without diabetes can prevent or slow the progress of diabetes *complications*. *Monitoring* blood sugar carefully can give people with diabetes many years of healthy, active life.

Words to Know

Complications: diseases or conditions that develop after or as a result of a main disease or condition.

Monitoring: watching, keeping track of, or checking.

Blood Sugar Monitoring

If you have diabetes, your blood-sugar monitor will be your new best friend. It's a way to be strong and take charge of your own health.

Blood-sugar monitors are small devices like the ones shown here. They measure your blood sugar levels from a small drop of your blood. Your doctor will tell you what your *target* blood-sugar range is.

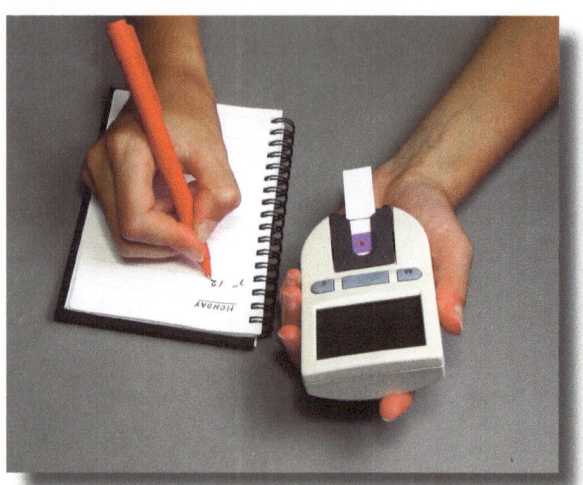

Words to Know

Target: what you want to achieve.

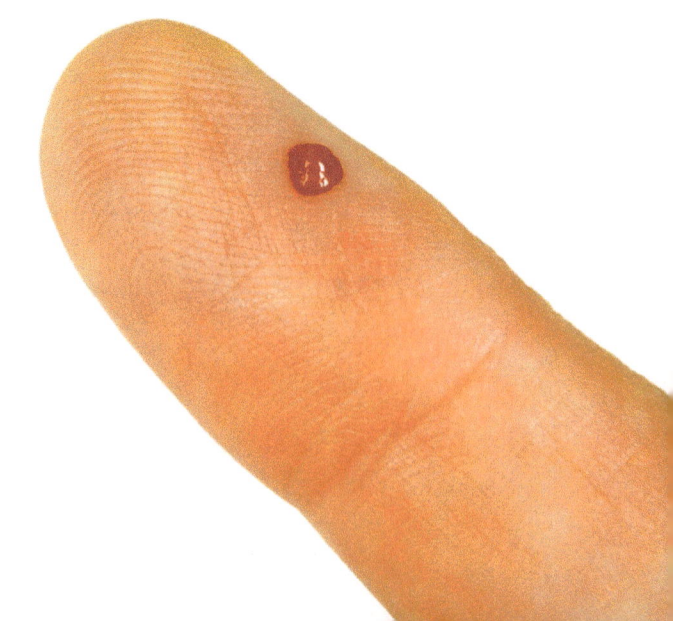

If you write down your blood-sugar numbers, you will have a record to show your doctor that will tell him how well your treatment is working and if anything needs to be changed.

How many times a day you need to test your blood-sugar level will depend on what type of diabetes you have. If you have type 1 diabetes, you will probably need to test your blood more often than if you have type 2 diabetes. Your doctor will give you a schedule that's right for you. Having to prick your finger so often may seem pretty awful at first—but it's really not so bad, and you'll get used to it soon.

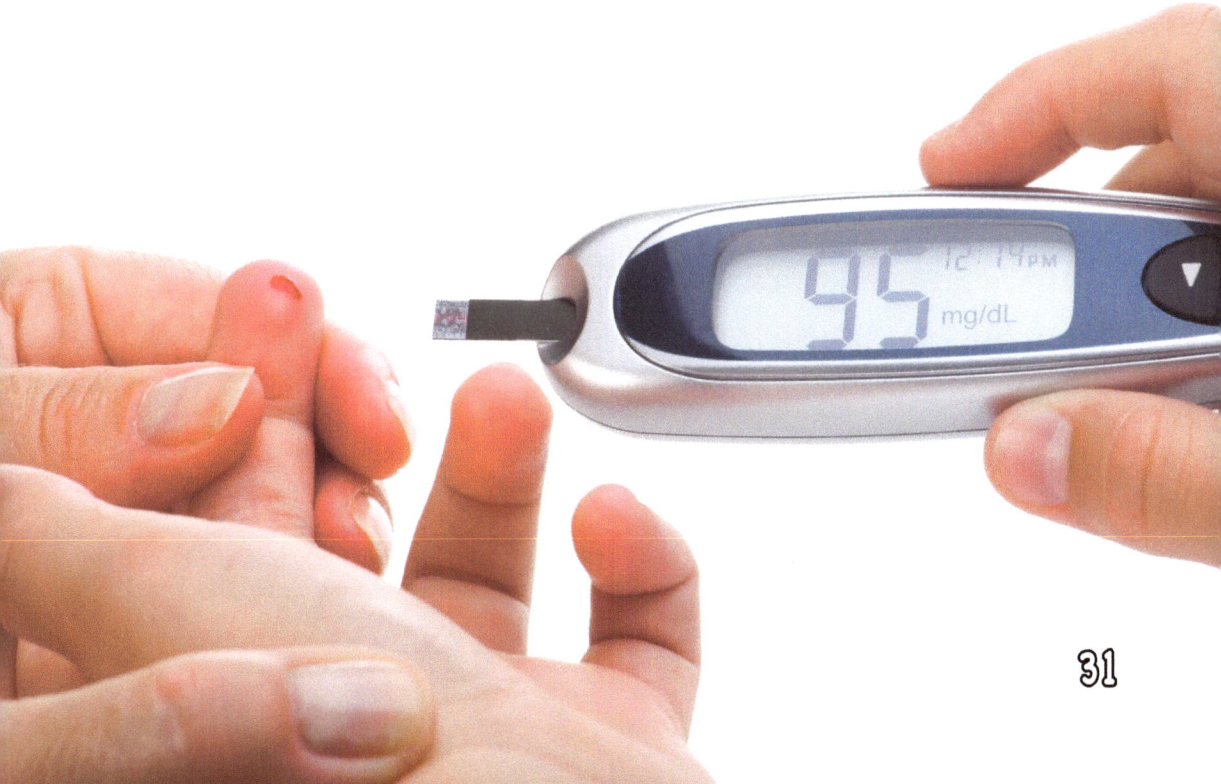

Hypo/Hyperglycemia

When your blood-sugar levels drop too low, it's called hypoglycemia. This means there's too much insulin in your blood and not enough sugar. It can make you feel shaky, clumsy, dizzy, and out of sorts. It happens if you take too much diabetes medicine, if you skip a meal or don't eat enough, if you exercise more without eating more, or if you drink alcohol. When people with diabetes have hypoglycemia, they need to eat or drink something sweet right away. It's easy to fix, but if ignored, it can lead to unconsciousness or *seizures*.

Hyperglycemia is just the opposite: it's when a person's blood sugar is too high. This can make a person feel thirsty and tired. It happens if someone with diabetes forgets to take medicine, eats too much of the wrong food, or doesn't exercise enough.

If you have diabetes and you discover you have hyperglycemia, you'll need to test your urine with one of the little strips shown on the left page. If the test shows you have something called *ketones* in your urine, you will need to see your doctor.

> **Words to Know**
>
> **Seizures:** sudden changes in behavior caused by cells within the brain that are not firing correctly.
>
> **Ketones:** the poisonous substance released when blood-sugar levels climb too high, and your body begins to break down your stored fat.

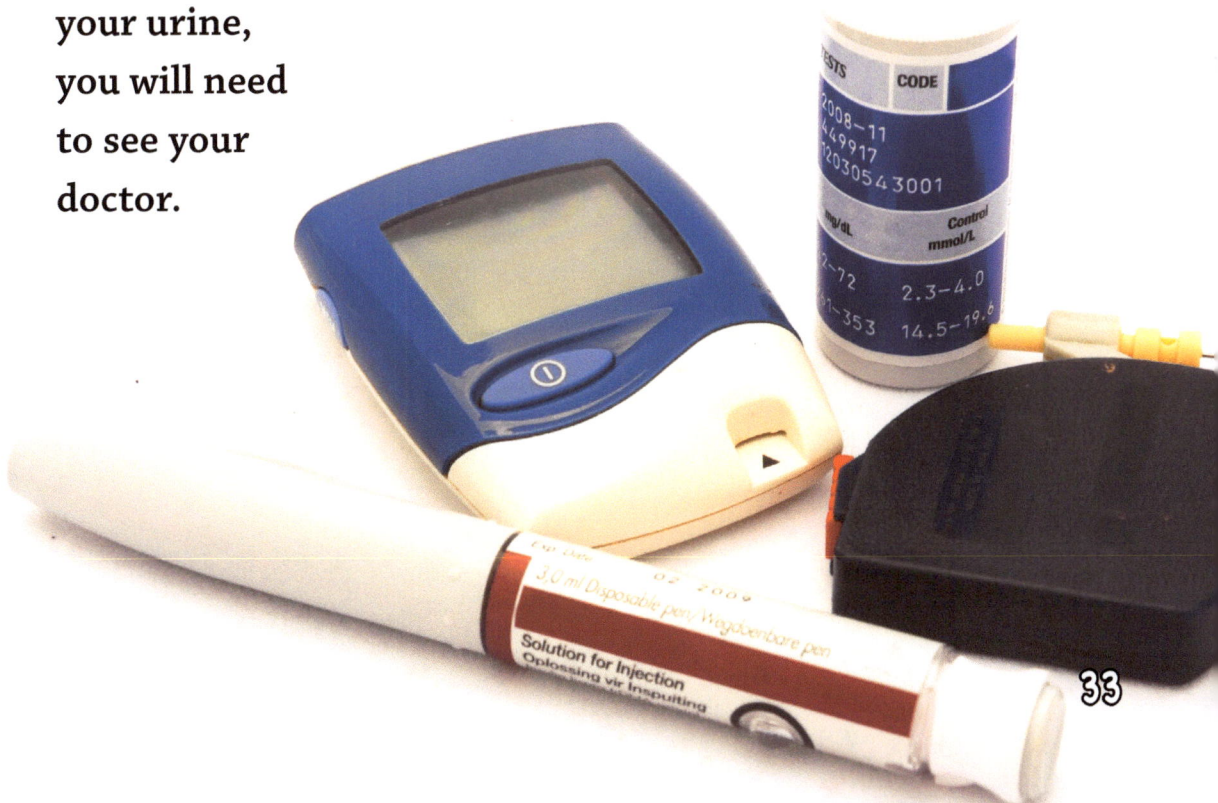

Diet and Exercise

The right diet and plenty of exercise helps control diabetes. People with type 2 diabetes may even be able to control the disease without medicine.

Words to Know

Fiber: the part of plant foods that your body can't digest. It's found in vegetables, fruits, and whole-grain breads and cereal.

When people have diabetes, they need to eat lots of high-*fiber* foods, like vegetables and fruits that aren't too sweet. They need to limit how many sweets, fats, and proteins they eat.

Exercise is also important, since it helps control weight and lowers blood-sugar levels. It also lowers a person's risk of heart disease, a condition common in people who have diabetes. Exercise can also help you feel better about yourself and increase your overall health.

Insulin Treatment

If you have type 2 diabetes, at first your doctor will probably try to control your disease with diet and exercise alone. But if your blood-sugar levels can't be controlled that way, or if you have type 1 diabetes, you will probably need to take some form of insulin.

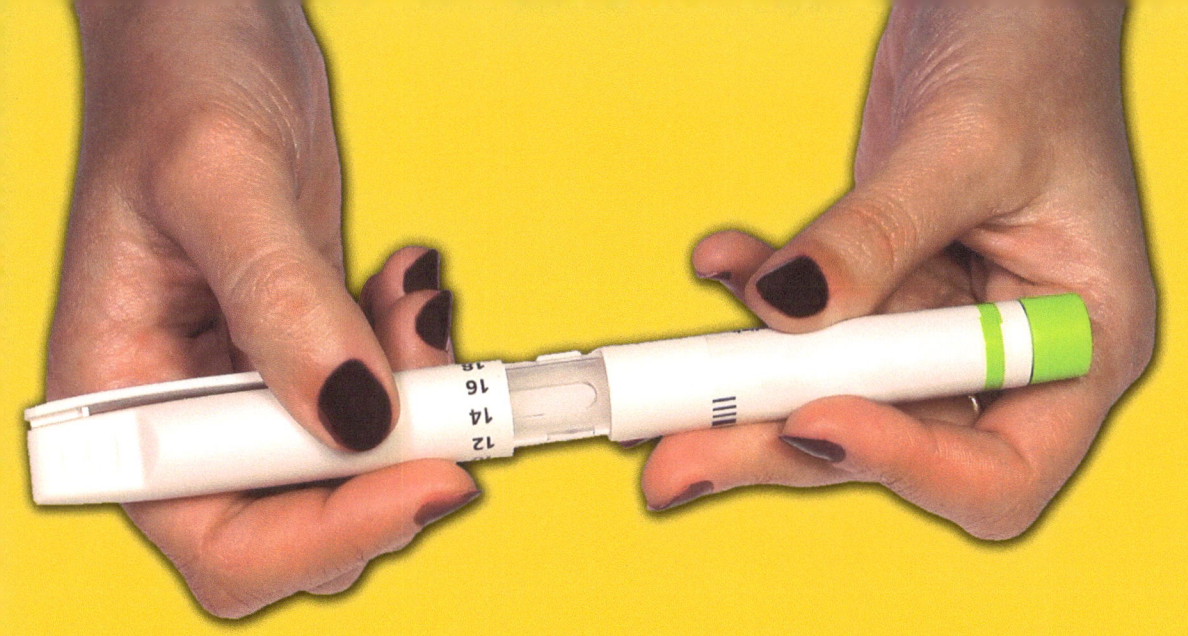

Many people with diabetes take insulin to control their blood sugar. Insulin cannot be taken by mouth because it would be destroyed by *digestion*, so there's no such thing as insulin pills.

There are many types of insulin. Some start working right away, some work more slowly, and some last a long time in a person's body. Your doctor will help you decide which kind is right for your condition and *lifestyle*.

Words to Know

Digestion: the process of breaking down food that takes place in your stomach and intestines.

Lifestyle: your way of life, including your values and personal habits.

Pills, Shots, Pumps

Many people with type 2 diabetes take diabetes pills (shown on the page to the right). These will only work for people whose pancreases still make some insulin, so they cannot help people with type 1 diabetes. Diabetes pills are not insulin. Instead, they help lower blood sugar in other ways.

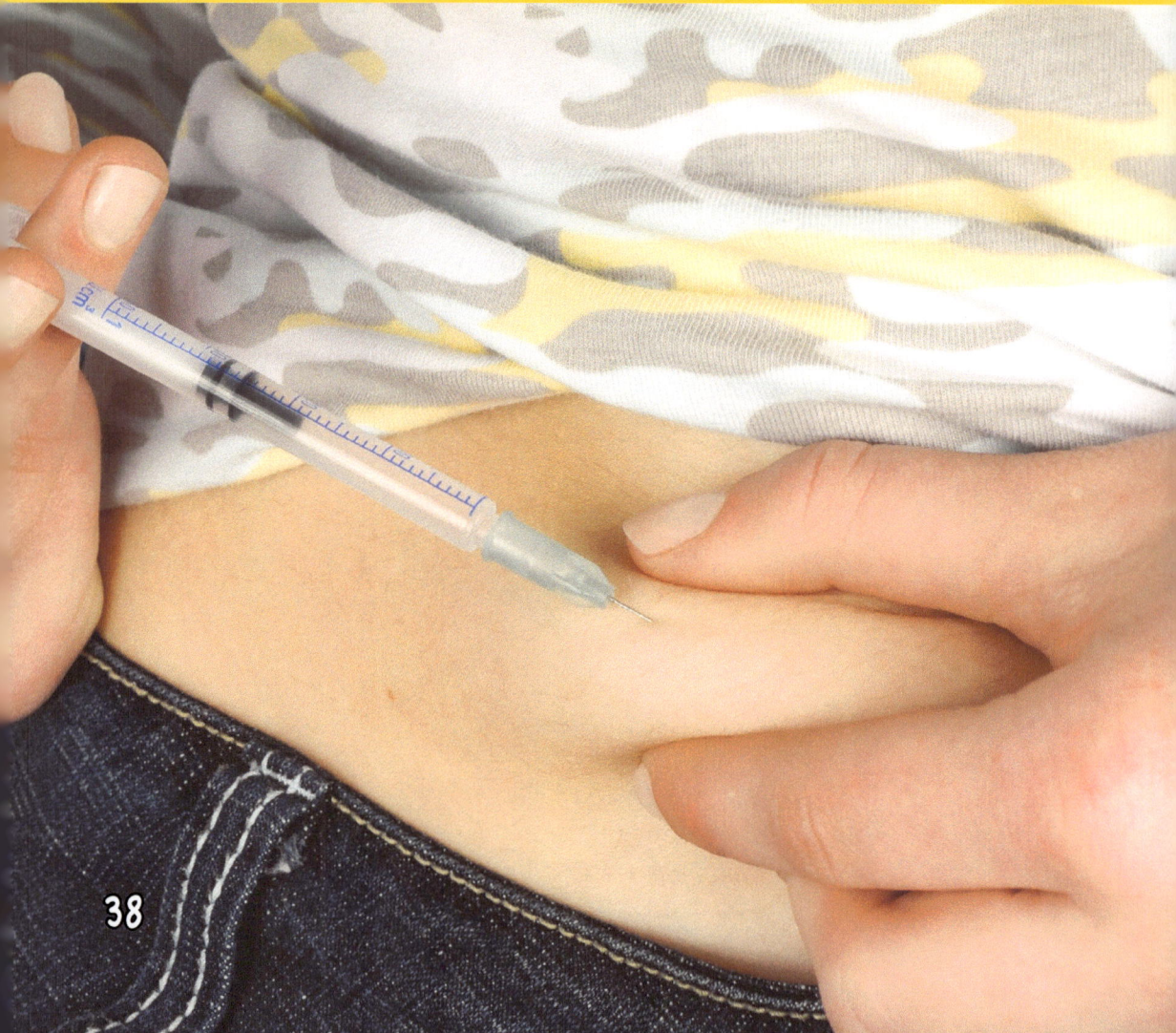

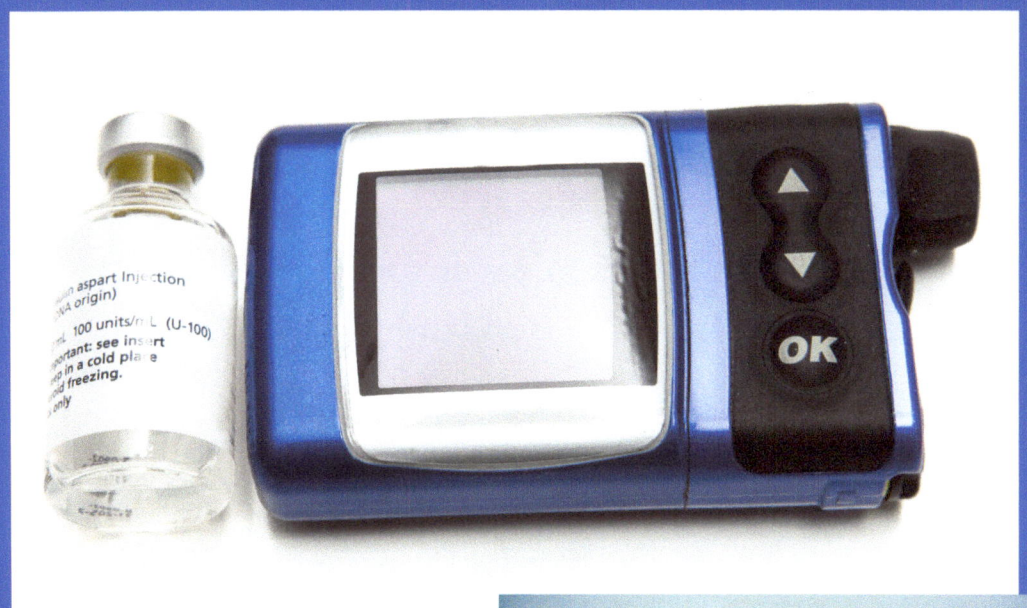

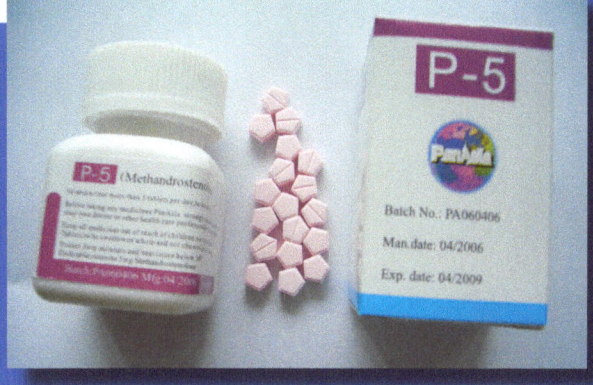

    Because insulin can't be swallowed, it has to be put right in your bloodstream. Most people who need insulin take insulin shots. Having to give yourself shots every day may seem scary, but insulin shots don't hurt that much because the needles are short and shots are placed into fatty tissue below the skin. An insulin pump (shown to the right) is another way to get insulin into your blood. It delivers insulin through a tube into your blood twenty-four hours a day, so you don't have to have shots.

Diabetic Shock

If people with diabetes monitor their blood sugar carefully, take their medication, and follow the correct diet, most of the time their disease won't interfere with their lives. But when something gets off balance in their lives—they go to a birthday party and eat the wrong foods, they forget to take their medicine because they're so busy, or they're upset about something and

their emotions get in the way of caring for themselves properly—then either hypoglycemia or hyperglycemia can occur. If not treated correctly right away, both of these conditions can lead to serious medical conditions, including diabetic shock.

People in diabetic shock can lose consciousness. They need medical care right away. Another condition that can be caused by diabetes is diabetic *coma*, a more serious condition. A candy or drink of fruit juice or soda can help a person with hypoglycemia, but if the person can't be roused, call your community's emergency number immediately.

Words to Know

Coma: a long period of deep unconsciousness.

Who Gets Diabetes?

Diabetes affects all types of people all around the world.
    If someone in your family has type 1 diabetes, your chances of getting this disease are greater, since doctors believe it is at least partly *hereditary*.

Type 2 diabetes, however, is more apt to occur to people who:

- are overweight
- carry fat around their waists
- are over forty-five
- don't exercise much
- have a family history of type 2 diabetes
- have high blood pressure

Sometimes people have a condition that is between "normal" and diabetes. Their blood sugar levels are higher than normal, but they aren't high enough to be considered diabetes. These people are at high risk of getting diabetes later in life. But diet and exercise can help.

Words to Know

Hereditary: tending to occur in families, passed down from parents to children through the body's genetic material.

Did You Know?

Type 2 diabetes used to be quite rare before middle age, but now affects more and more young people who are overweight. Being overweight, even as a child or teenager, also puts you at risk of developing diabetes as an adult.

Diabetes Triggers

Did You Know?

Scientists have found that although type 1 diabetes is mostly hereditary, it also is triggered by three things. One is related to cold weather: type 1 diabetes develops more often in winter than summer and is more common in places with cold climates. Another trigger might be a virus (a type of germ) that has only mild effects on most people but triggers type 1 diabetes in others. And last, early diet may also play a role: type 1 diabetes is less common in people who were breastfed and in those who first ate solid foods at later ages.

Like type 1 diabetes, type 2 diabetes can sometimes run in families—but certain things *trigger* type 2 diabetes (whether or not you have a family history of this disease). The two most important triggers are sugary foods and foods that are high in fat. Eating a fast-food diet puts you at risk!

Words to Know

Trigger: cause something to happen somewhere else.

Obesity and Diabetes

Obesity is a growing problem around the world. As people in more and more countries begin to eat more like Americans—lots of fast food, lots of large portions, lots of *processed* sugars and flours, lots of fats—more and more people are putting on weight. Being overweight is a serious problem. It's not a question of what you look like—it's a question of how healthy you are. Being overweight or obese puts you at risk for a lot of other serious health conditions, including diabetes.

Words to Know

Processed: treated in some way (referring to food) with chemicals or broken down with machines into smaller pieces that are less healthy for your body.

Did You Know?

Scientists believe that fat cells in your body may release a hormone that makes your body resist insulin. This would explain why people with more fat cells would have higher blood-sugar levels.

Scientists are still studying the link between diabetes and obesity. They're not sure WHY being obese makes you more likely to develop type 2 diabetes—but they know it does. Losing weight lowers blood-sugar levels. And it makes people less apt to develop diabetes in the first place.

Genetics and Diabetes

In most cases of type 1 diabetes, people need to inherit *risk factors* from both parents. These are passed on through their genes.

Genes are lined up on chromosomes, long, thread-like spirals like the one shown on these pages. Chromosomes come in pairs, and there are hundreds, sometimes thousands, of genes on one chromosome. Each of your biological parents has two copies of each of their genes, and each of your parents pass along just one copy to make up the genes you have. These make the blueprint

> **Words to Know**
>
> **Risk factors:** traits or conditions that make it more likely a person will develop an illness.

> **Did You Know?**
>
> Each cell in your body contains 25,000 to 35,000 genes.

for who you are. They carry the information that tells your cells how to behave. They're responsible for the color of your eyes, how tall you are, how smart you are, and sometimes, what diseases you have—like diabetes. Scientists haven't found an exact gene that causes diabetes, but they have found groups of genes that seem to be responsible for the condition.

Diabetes Research

Scientists are constantly trying to find newer and better ways to treat diabetes. Shown here is a tiny insulin sensor that attaches to the skin with an adhesive patch. It constantly tracks the wearer's glucose levels and transmits it to a device about the size of a cell phone—all without needing to prick your finger every day!

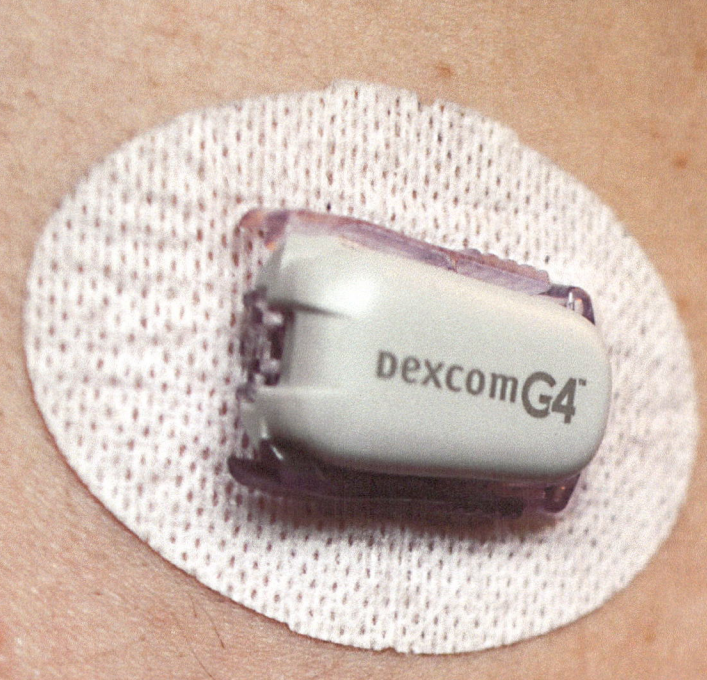

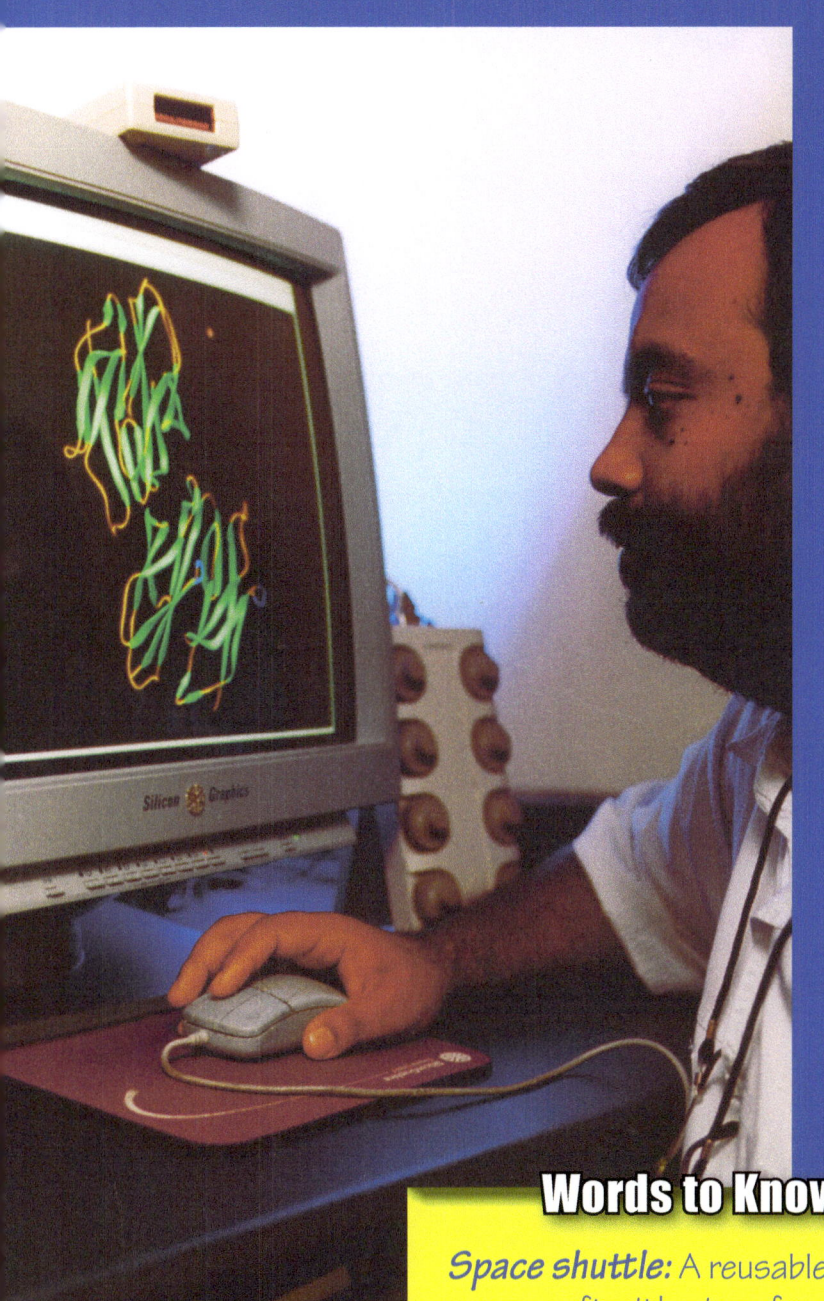

Even the U.S. space program is playing a role in insulin research. Here a researcher studies new insulin "blueprints" made from crystals grown on board NASA's *space shuttle*.

Words to Know

Space shuttle: A reusable spacecraft with wings for controlled descent in the atmosphere, designed to transport astronauts between Earth and an orbiting space station. They were also used to launch and retrieve satellites.

What Is the World Doing About Diabetes?

Diabetes is a global *epidemic.* It affects people around the world. People who live in countries with less money often have fewer treatment options. Because they don't receive regular medical care, they may not even know they have diabetes.

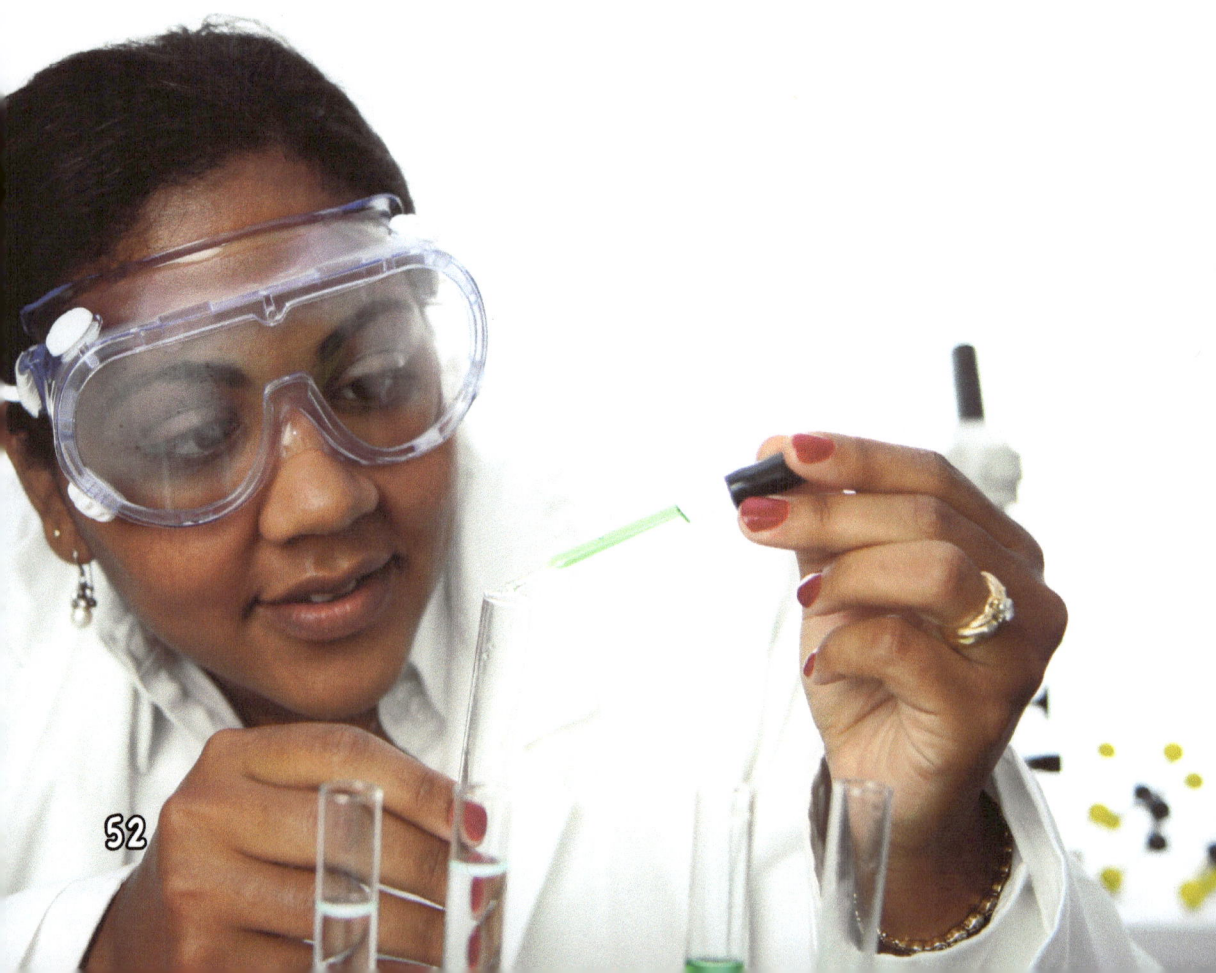

Words to Know

Epidemic: a disease that affects large numbers of people.

International: involving more than one country.

Did You Know?

Diabetes causes about 5 percent of all deaths globally each year.

80 percent of people with diabetes live in low- and middle-income countries.

Unless the world takes action, diabetes deaths are likely to increase by more than 50 percent in the next ten years.

The United Nations (UN) is an *international* organization made up of the world's countries, all working together to help people who live around the globe. In 2007, the UN set aside November 14 as World Diabetes Day. This is a special day to bring more attention to this disease. The UN is working hard to educate the people of the world about how they can prevent and treat diabetes.

Education and research offer the most hope—and neither can be carried out without money. Individuals, organizations, and nations are also working to battle diabetes. By raising money for diabetes research and education, the people of the world are fighting diabetes.

What Can You Do?

You can make healthy decisions right now that will help you either prevent diabetes or live with diabetes.

Eat lots of fruits and vegetables. If you pick from a rainbow of colors, you will be more apt to get the *variety* of vitamins and minerals you need. Eat whole-grain foods. Choose lean meats and low-fat dairy products. Limit how many sugary drinks and foods you eat. Control your portion sizes (how much you eat in one sitting). And don't forget to exercise!

Words to Know

Variety: an assortment of different things.

Real Kids

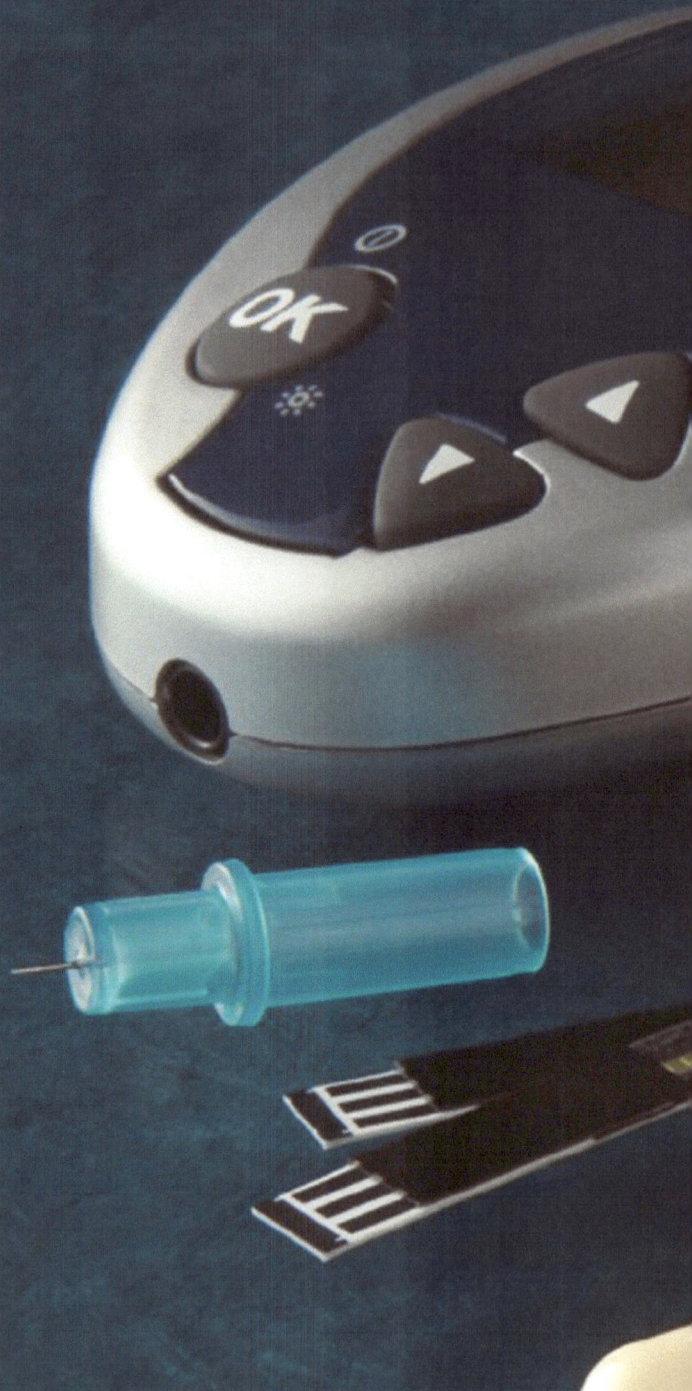

When Cory Dunham was three years old, his mother noticed that he was always asking for a drink—and he needed to go to the bathroom constantly. His mom thought he might have an infection in his *urinary tract*, but when she took him to the doctor, it turned out that he had type 1 diabetes instead.

Cory can barely remember now what it was like to not have diabetes.

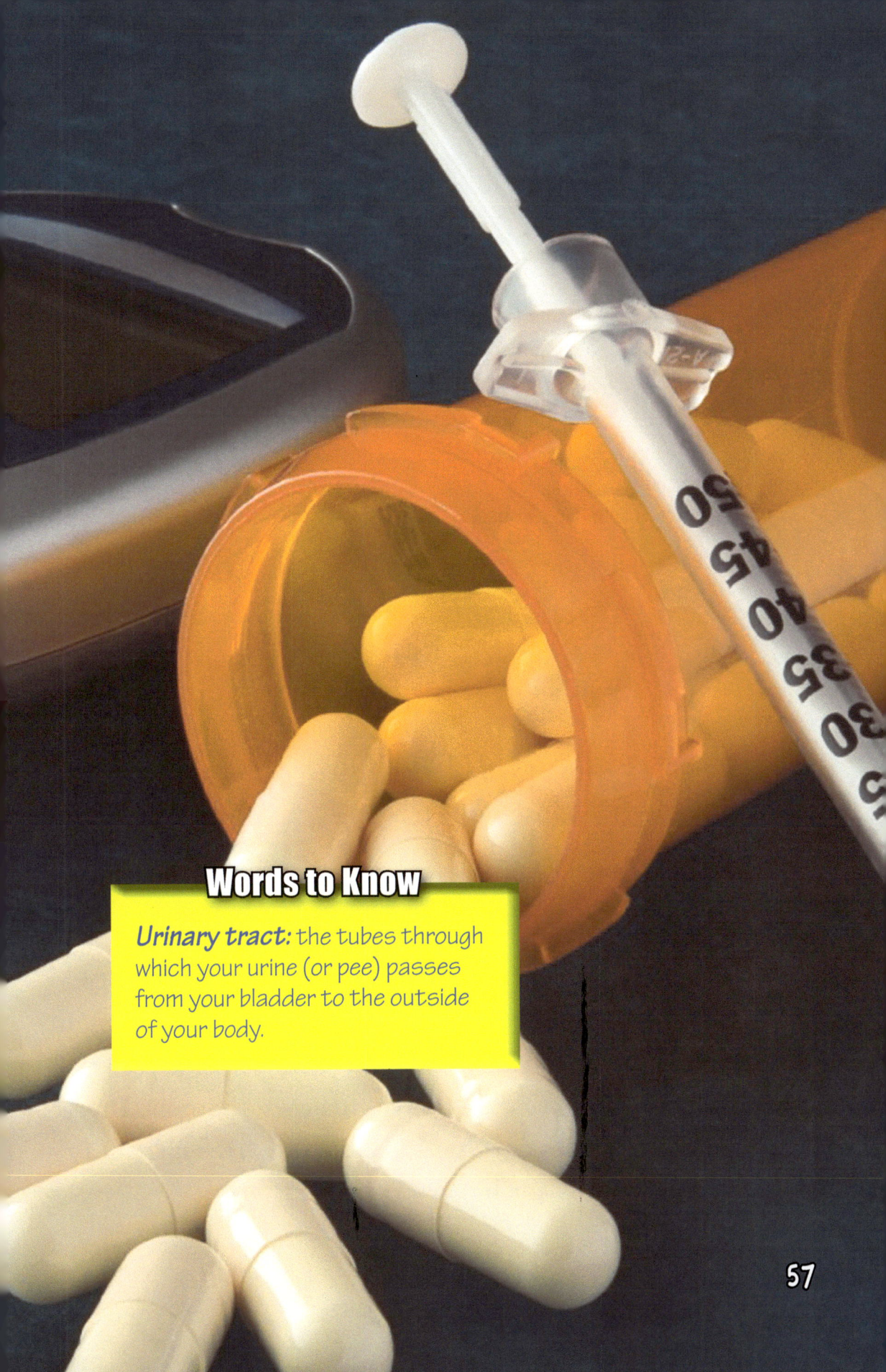

Words to Know

Urinary tract: the tubes through which your urine (or pee) passes from your bladder to the outside of your body.

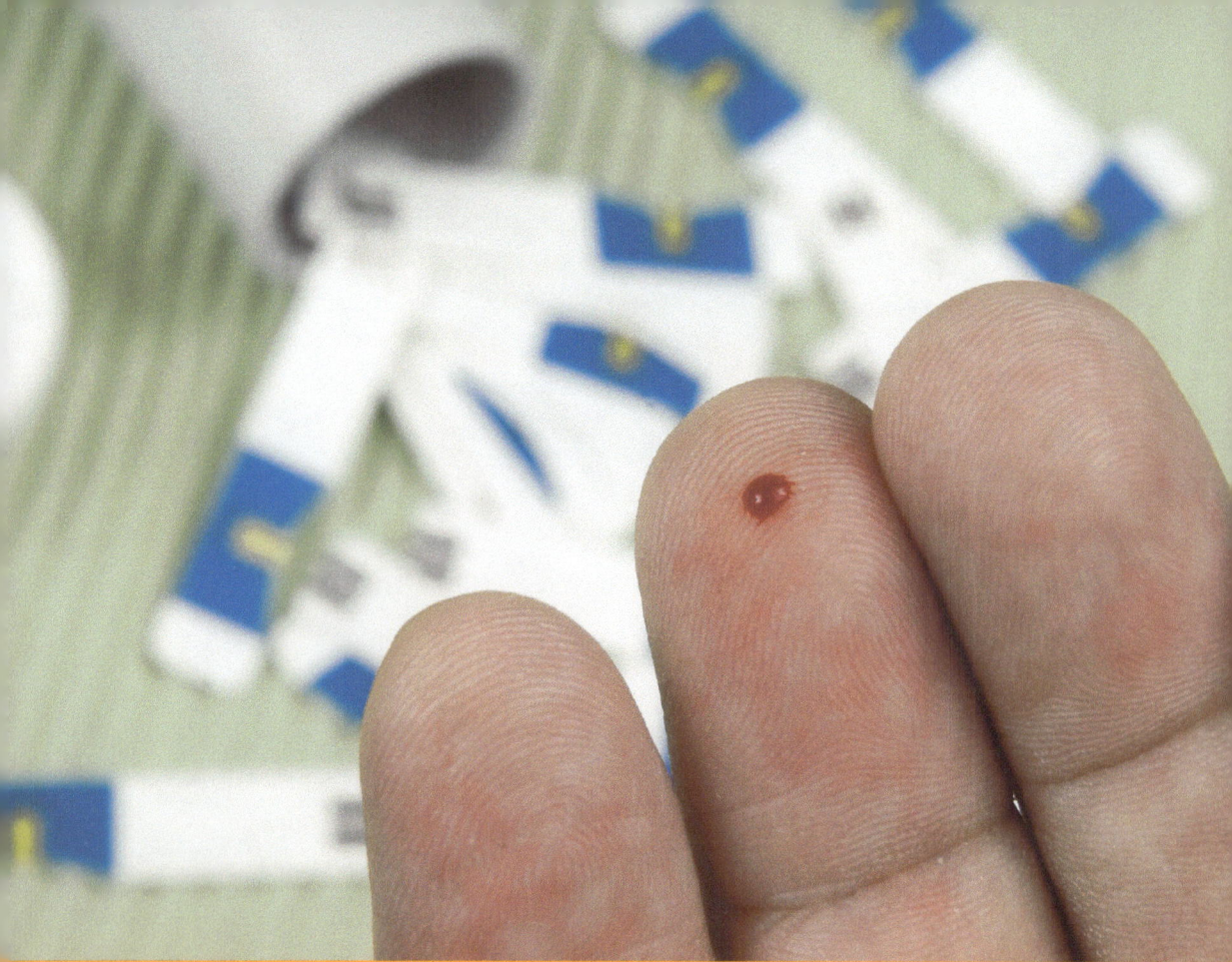

Words to Know

Faint: without strength and likely to fall down.

When he was five, he learned how to give himself shots. He was really excited about that, the way some kids might be excited about learning to tie their shoes. That year he also started going to diabetes camp every summer. There, he got to know lots of other kids like him. He learned how other children his age handled diabetes.

Cory is twelve now. Checking his blood sugar three times a day is just a normal part of life for him. Giving himself shots is something he doesn't think twice about. Eating the right foods isn't as easy for him, though, especially when he's with his friends. One time he got in trouble with his mom because he drank too much soda at a party and ended up with ketones in his urine. His doctor yelled at him too. And a few times he's forgotten to eat because he was having such a good time playing ball with his friends—and he's ended up feeling *faint* and dizzy, having to drink some orange juice right away.

Most of the time, though, Cory feels proud of how he handles his disease all on his own. He's looking forward to the new inventions and medicines he knows scientists will come up with in the years to come that will make living with diabetes easier—but in the meantime, he doesn't think about it all that much. He's too busy with school and friends to worry about diabetes.

Find Out More

These websites will tell you more about diabetes.

American Academy of Family Physicians: Diabetes
familydoctor.org/familydoctor/en/diseases-conditions/diabetes.html

American Diabetes Association
www.diabetes.org

Harvard School of Public Health: Type 2 Diabetes
www.hsph.harvard.edu/nutritionsource/more/type-2-diabetes

International Diabetes Federation
www.idf.org

MedlinePlus Diabetes
www.nlm.nih.gov/medlineplus/diabetes.html

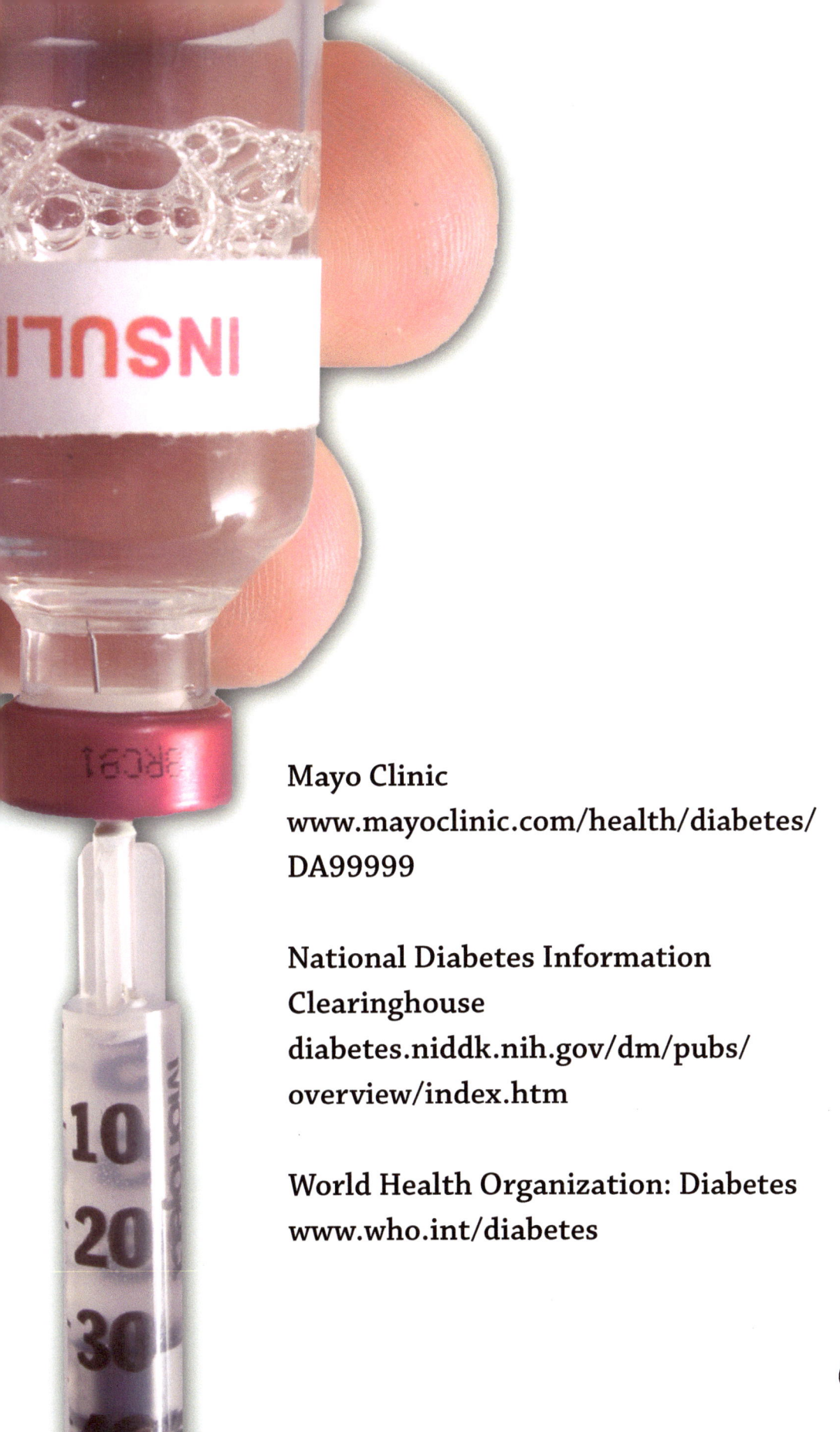

Mayo Clinic
www.mayoclinic.com/health/diabetes/
DA99999

National Diabetes Information
Clearinghouse
diabetes.niddk.nih.gov/dm/pubs/
overview/index.htm

World Health Organization: Diabetes
www.who.int/diabetes

Index

blood sugar 13, 16, 23, 25, 27, 29–33, 35–38, 40, 46–47
blood test 26–27

diabetes 8–9, 19–25, 27–40, 42–50, 52–54
    juvenile 20–21
    Type 1 21, 24, 27, 31, 38, 42, 44–45, 48
    Type 2 21–24, 27, 31, 34, 36, 38, 43, 45, 47
diabetic coma 41
diabetic shock 40–41

exercise, 32–26, 43, 55

family 42–43, 45
    history 43, 45
fat 14, 22, 25, 33, 35, 39, 43, 45–46, 55

genes 48–49
glucose 9–10, 13, 16, 22

hyperglycemia 32–33, 41
hypoglycemia 32, 41

insulin 9, 14–16, 18–19, 21–23, 25, 32, 36–39, 46, 50–51

ketone 33

obesity 23, 46–47
organ 9, 13–15, 53
overweight 43, 46

pancreas 9, 14–16, 21, 38
pump 39, 50

research 50–51, 53
risk 35, 43, 45–46, 48

seizure 32–33
sugar 9–10, 12–14, 16, 18–19, 23–25, 27, 29–33, 35–38, 40, 45–47, 55

urine 9, 33

Picture Credits

Alden Chadwick | Flickr Creative Commons: p 50

Charleson, C.: p. 35

Dreamstime:
AlphaSpirit: pp. 48–49
Anetta: pp. 26–27
Angelogive: pp. 8–9
Aniram: pp. 12–13
Atman: p. 38
BeckyAbell: p. 20
CB34inc: p. 11
Celsopupo: pp. 28–29, 36–37, 58–59
Devonyu: p. 45
Hdcphoto: p. 39
Icefields: p. 11
Kivig: p. 10–11
Liens: p. 41
Pazham: p. 34
Photowitch: p. 44
Razvanjp: p. 31
Rmarmion: pp. 52–53, 54–55
Robeo: p. 19
Ronfromyork: p. 30
Sansubba: pp. 22–23
Tobkatrina: p. 21
Traveling-Light: pp. 42–43
Westacott, Eliot: p. 25
White, E.J.: p. 24

iStockphotos
Cano, Richard: pp. 58–59
Stafford, Dawna: pp. 46–47
NASA: pp. 18, 51
National Institutes of Health: pp. 14–15, 16, 17

To the best knowledge of the publisher, all other images are in the public domain. If any image has been inadvertently uncredited, please notify Village Earth Press, Vestal, New York 13850, so that rectification can be made for future printings.

About the Author

Rae Simons has written many books for young adults and children. She lives with her family in New York State in the U.S.

About the Consultant

Elise DeVore Berlan, MD, MPH, FAAP, is a faculty member of the Division of Adolescent Health at Nationwide Children's Hospital and an Assistant Professor of Clinical Pediatrics at the Ohio State University College of Medicine. She completed her fellowship in adolescent medicine at Children's Hospital Boston and obtained a master's degree in public health at the Harvard School of Public Health. Dr. Berlan completed her residency in pediatrics at the Children's Hospital of Philadelphia, where she also served an additional year as chief resident. She received her medical degree from the University of Iowa College of Medicine.

www.ingramcontent.com/pod-product-compliance
Lightning Source LLC
Chambersburg PA
CBHW061358090426
42743CB00002B/51